# THE FURTHER ADVENTURES OF PHIL

## OF PHIL

By Susan G. Berman

For Geneva

## ACKNOWLEDGEMENTS

For my husband, Jeff for being a good doggy daddy.  To my mom, Alberta for being a willing gramma to all my canine companions. And to our vet Dr. Boschen and his staff for helping all our doggos live as long and healthy lives as possible.

# FORWARD

We lived in a rural area of Springfield, Missouri. We had a small bungalow that sat on two acres, all of which was fenced.

After living there for about six months, I thought we needed a dog. We had the perfect yard. It was fenced. There was shelter and shade and lots of areas to explore. Our backyard could be the ultimate dog park.

We didn't need to go looking for a dog, though. They all came to us!

Trudy was the first. She showed up one day in the middle of winter and stuck around. She was about a year-old border collie X at the time. At the time this was written, she had just turned eighteen and still kicking.

Phoebe showed up a few months after Trudy made her introductions. My husband found her shivering in the yard, so he brought her in, warmed her up and she lived with us for about twelve years. She was thought to be a terrier of some sort. I considered her a terrorer!

A year after Phoebe made her grand entrance, we took in a baby girl Beagle that kept coming up to the house. We brought her in, cleaned her up, and named her Phannie. She was about 9 months old, and the sweet little girl lived for almost twelve years.

A year after Phannie adopted us, my

husband adopted a nine-month-old lab puppy from a coworker. We named her Phred. She was smart, funny, playful, sweet and a gentle dog. She lived to be about fifteen.

A few months after adopting Phred, I rescued a two-year old doodle-something-or-other. His name was Brutus who lived to be about twelve. He was a kind and gentle soul. He *really* enjoyed the company of Phil in his last couple of years.

Phrancis was adopted as a companion for Phil shortly after Brutus passed away. She was a nine-month-old puppy when we welcomed her home. She would become Phil's shadow and constant canine companion.

At one time, there were six dogs living with us. Currently there are two and a half.

These stories are shared from my twisted perspectives, unique personal experiences and humorous life observations with and about my canine companions.

Phil saved me!

# WE SHALL CALL HIM PHIL

A couple years ago, there was a male beagle hanging around the neighborhood who apparently had nowhere else to go. We already had five dogs, which was probably the reason he came to us. He seemed to want to come inside the gate and play with the others.

I'd let him in and he would play, jump and run around for about thirty minutes until he got bored and wanted to be let out. This went on multiple times a day for a couple of weeks.

On a cold, wet and windy evening, long after it had gotten dark, there was a knock on our door. No one knocks on our door during the daytime, let alone during the evening,

so me and my husband were a bit startled.
We opened the door to find our neighbors,
both of them, and a familiar little dog on
the other end of a leash. They asked us if
the dog was ours. Because we have so many
already, they just assumed he was.

Well, it did not take but a hot minute and
a silent look at each other before we said,
"Sure, he's ours."

They handed him over and that is how Phil
came to be one of us!

# AND HE RAN.

I had mail-ordered a life jacket for Phil to help keep him inside the fence. We have pig-wire fencing all around the yard and the holes are bigger. The jackets help bulk up the dogs so they could not easily squeeze through the fence. We used jackets on the other dogs when they first became part of our family as a training tool. After repeatedly trying to get through the fence and failing, the dogs eventually gave up. But the size of the holes would prove to not be a problem for Phil.

I fitted Phil with a brand new bright yellow jacket and for the first time in days, let him off his lead to run free in the yard with the other dogs. Well, run free he did.

He found a breach in the fence and the little fucker ran.

I was quite dismayed, a little pissed, and sad as well. This was supposed to work.

"Damn it, Phil!"

I walked the yard, all two acres of it, looking for Phil in his bright yellow jacket. Walked the neighborhood. Nothing. Nada.

So, I waited for my husband to get home from work.

A few minutes after he got home, we were driving around the neighborhood. We even trespassed on some private property that was on the other side of our back fence in our search. But still no sign of him.

I had felt bad for Phil not knowing where he was or if he was okay. I had a restless night.

The next morning, I kept an eye open for him as I looked out windows and stepped onto the front porch. No Phil in his bright yellow jacket.

Later that morning, I spotted him. He was at the front fence in the company of a long-legged, long blond hair bitch. He had ditched his bright yellow jacket, but he seemed all right and quite happy with his new girlfriend.

I called out to him, but he was not paying me any attention. His focus was all on his new girlfriend. She really was quite pretty. They both took off down the street.

*Damn it! Once a scoundrel always a scoundrel,* I thought to myself. This was what he was used to, and it would be difficult to change his behavior.

Or so I thought.

That afternoon I was sitting in the living room, a little sad. The other dogs were enjoying their afternoon snooze-fest and all was quiet in the house. Jeff had gotten home and as he walked in, he kept glancing down.

It was Phil! Phil had come home! Sans bright yellow jacket and sans new girlfriend. But he was home.

Later that afternoon Jeff, the dogs and I walked the fence line and repaired several spots through which Phil could possibly escape.

In the meantime, Phil was put back on his twenty-five-foot lead. At least until he got neutered, which was just a couple of days later.

Meanwhile, Phil got a new replacement jacket. It was bright pink and I made sure to get his name, address and phone number written on it just in case he got out again. We were doing everything we could to convince Phil that this would be a great home and he could be quite happy here.
Even if he had to wear a bright-pink jacket.

# COATS OF MANY COLORS

When I first decided to give Phil a chance, I outfitted him in a bright yellow jacket. Well, that lasted exactly one day. He had escaped and ditched it somewhere, never to be found.

I ordered another jacket. He got it caught on something and tore off the top handle, losing the leash clip in the process, Not only had he rolled in cow shit, crap-staining the hell out of it, he ran through some brush and ripped it in several places. In one day!

So, I ordered another in bright pink. That one lasted about a week. He managed to rip the handle off, tear a hole in its side, and chewed off a strap.

Phil's next but not-so-final jacket was neon green. He managed to roll in something vile, again. Even after it was washed three times, the putrid stink would not come out. We had no choice but to toss it and we ordered him another jacket. Safety orange would be the next color.

That hound was hard on his jackets!

# DOG SHIT

For sixteen years, my husband and I have

lived in our little bungalow set on two semi-

wooded, semi-wild and green-grassed fenced

acres in a rural community of Springfield.

For the better part of these sixteen years,

we have owned dogs—multiple dogs. For

sixteen years, I have traipsed all over these

two acres without a care,

and for sixteen years,

I have NEVER EVER

stepped in dog shit.

Then Phil came along!

Now, we already had a

male dog, but he had been neutered before I

took him in, so we didn't have to go through

'the cone of shame, leashed walks, and being hooked on a lead' phase.

Well, Phil was whole when he came to us, and until he wasn't so whole anymore, he required daily leashed walking, along with lead time and house time, which was an important part of his daily routine.

Now, I generally wore a crappy ass pair of slippers around the house and yard. I even did some outdoor gardening in these crappy ass slippers. So it goes without saying that I would wear my crappy ass slippers to take Phil for walks. Day and night, I took Phil for walks all around the two-acre yard.

Before Phil, NO STEPPING IN DOG SHIT!
After Phil, STEPPING IN DOG SHIT!

And in my crappy ass slippers! No more could I wear them around the house! Let alone around the yard. They were ruined.

So I decided to go online and order a pair of rubber boots for traipsing around the yard and if I stepped in dog shit, I could just hose the boots off, therein saving my new slippers for around the house.

Boots were delivered. I was excited so I slipped my feet in. I hooked up Phil to a long leash and away we went, traipsing all over two acres, running through thick layers of crunchy leaves, following squirrel and deer scents, and having not a care in the world. We were outside for a good hour or so exploring the back forty, the front forty, the east and west forty, not paying any attention to where we were stepping, and -

NOT ONCE DID I STEP IN DOG SHIT!

# OFF THE LEAD

When Phil was fitted with his new hot-pink jacket it was time, once again, to let him off the lead. It took him a hot minute to realize he wasn't tied up and wouldn't be jerked back after twenty paces. And then he was gone.

I ran with him, leash in hand and treats in my pocket, and followed him all around the yard. I had to leash him up only once to pull him away from the fence between us and the neighbors and their dogs and redirect his attention toward something quieter. He then caught up with the other doggos patrolling the fence line and he had a ball. He ran through brush, over logs, under logs, sniffing and snortling and wagging both tail and body. And he bellowed. And he howled. And he snorted and he grunted. I followed him and did my best to keep up.

He did find a small breach in the fence but that was easily fixed on the spot. We had learned to keep zip ties in our pockets when we ventured out to the way-back forty just in case the fence needed mending.

We covered the east, west, north and south forty, and
NOT ONCE DID I STEP IN ANY DOG SHIT!

# WHEN THE DEVIL DOG CAME OUT TO PLAY

Wow, Phil!

For the most part Phil was an incredibly good boy. He was super smart, affectionate, cuddly and a fairly mellow, laid back young fellow.

But—there's always a but!  On occasion, the Devil Dog would come out in Phil and he'd turn into the Tazmanian Devil himself. He nipped at our heels, bit at our toes, tugged on our pant hems, chewed on blankets, dragged towels around the house, ran off with our shoes and socks, and ate the corner cabinet, just to name a few crimes. He even

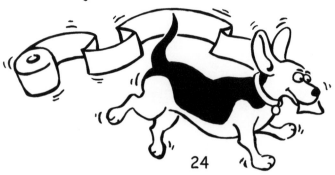

grabbed the end piece of the toilet paper and ran through the house as it unrolled.

OMG, on that particular day, he was out of control. He got super agitated and worked himself into a lather and play-bit me on the thigh and my arm. He attacked the other dogs by jumping on them, barking at them and just being Out. Of. Control.

It took some rather harsh reprimands to get him to stop. There were lots of 'nos' and 'no Phils' said that day. I used the spray bottle a lot.

When he finally collapsed that evening, no doubt from sheer exhaustion Jeff and I sat back, looked at each other and were like, "What the fuck was that?"

The next day, Phil woke up a different

dog. He wasn't jumping on us. He wasn't

terrorizing the other dogs. He wasn't eating

the cabinets. He didn't bite anyone. He was

a totally different Phil. He was a chilled Phil.

A few days later, just a little bit of

the Devil Dog came out in Phil. He was

reprimanded swiftly and sternly. But only

once. He was learning.

The next day he did remarkedly well. He got

a little too excited and only tried once to

bite my leg. But a swift, "NO PHIL!" stopped

his jaws from connecting with my flesh. He

was definitely a work in progress.

And for just a little while, he would be

known as a Devil Dog in a Pink Vest!

# THE BEST DAY EVER!

 On a cold and wet morning, I bundled up in my battered plaid barn jacket, pulled on my knit cap, and pulled on my boots. My chore that day was to slog across the yard and mend an area of fence that Phil had escaped through the previous day.

When I was done zip-tying the fence, I followed him all around the fence line to make sure he couldn't find another breach. To my relief, he did not.

Throughout that day, I looked out the

windows and doors and checked to see where he was in the yard. He managed to stay in the yard all that day, but not without trying to escape. Boy, he tried, but so far, the fence held him in. The jacket was doing its job.

What a bonus this was for me as I really didn't like having to bundle up to go outside in frigid weather to search for a dog and mend a fence.

That evening he was sacked out. Hard! Incredibly Hard!

Oh, he had experienced the sweet taste of freedom and it showed with his every snore and snort. He dreamt of many more days of total unrestrained freedom.

# THE TRIALS OF ELDER DOGGOS

One night around 9:00, I heard a commotion coming from the bedroom. It sounded like furniture being tossed about. I got in the room and poor Phred was having another seizure. It was the third one (that we knew of) and the second seizure in as many weeks. That night was particularly bad. It lasted about ten to fifteen minutes. She had lost control of her bladder and the frothing of the mouth was intense. The aftermath was even more frightening. When she came out of her seizure, she was extremely disoriented. She didn't know where she was. Nor who we were. The other dogs seemed unfamiliar to her. It would be over an hour before she realized where she was and calmed down.

The sad thing was there was nothing we could do when the seizures hit. We just did our best to comfort, talk softly to and soothe the great beast.

The vet eventually put Phred on meds to help control the seizures.

# THE NEW GPS TRACKER

Until Jeff was physically well enough to mend the fences properly, or until we saved enough money to buy a new fence—which wasn't going to happen any time real soon—a GPS unit sounded like a really good option, so we decided to put one to the Phil test.

The device was offered through our cellphone service for the introductory price of $10, plus $10 a month for the actual tracking service. It was simply a cool gadget. There was an option for live tracking so you could see on your phone where the dogs were traveling around the yard for up to a two-mile radius. You could even track how many steps your dog took that day.

We attached the tracker unit which was about an inch in diameter to one of the straps on his jacket.  It was out of the way of his movements and wouldn't get snagged on anything.

A few weeks went by and there was no escaping.

However, Phil STILL did not go out without wearing his jacket outfitted with a freshly charged GPS unit for the next few months.

# A JAILBREAK, A RECKONING,
# A RELEASE

One morning, I decided to let Phil loose in the backyard armed in his hot-pink jacket with a charged GPS unit attached.

He breached the fence only once that day and was quickly apprehended and brought back home. When the dog breached the boundaries previously set up as a safe zone, an alarm sounded on the phone.

After a brief discussion with Phil, rather a lecture, he was once again released into the wilds of the Berman property, still outfitted in his hot-pink jacket and a fully charged GPS unit.

He ran amok for hours.

He spotted a squirrel and ran after it so fast and furious, he was halfway up the trunk of the tree before he realized where he was.

He bayed and barked at the neighbor's dogs and pleaded for someone to come open the gate so he could venture even farther than the whole 9,900 square foot dog park that was already at his disposal.

Go figure. Beagles!

He stayed in the safe zone the rest of the day. He would come inside to say howdy in his whole-body-wiggling way, then jet back out to continue his adventure.

He was happy being a free dog at last!

# HE'S MINE, ALL MINE! MINE, MINE, MINE, MINE, MINE

Young Phil had made his mark on this family.
He had settled comfortably into the routine
the other doggos had set for themselves.
It didn't take him long to learn the rules,
like not peeing on the fridge or pooping in
the house.

Of all the dogs, Brutus was most definitely
Phil's favorite buddy. Brutus was a fifty pound,
long legged, skinny build, and wild hair doodle.
He was about ten and the youngest of the pack
until Phil came along. A very good-natured and
tolerant Brutus put up with a lot from Phil. He
was undeniably patient when Phil pulled on his
fur but didn't hesitate in putting the youngster
in his place if he got out of hand, like biting too

hard. Brutus was the one who taught young Phil the importance of good grooming.

They played together quite a LOT. They hunted and patrolled the yard together. They hung out on Mom's front porch, looking out at the yard, enjoying the warmth of the sun and planning their next moves.

But Brutus had something about him that Phil was not-so-secretly attracted to. It was his penis. Phil was constantly licking on  Brutus' groin. There were times when Brutus would run away, sit, and cross his legs to keep Phil away from his penis. Other times Brutus would just stand there, with a big ol' smile on his face, enjoying Phil's affections.

# THE SLIPPER INCIDENT!

The other night around 7 or so, I was in my PJs and pink robe. I had taken off my slippers and placed them on the floor next to my chair. I was a lounging lizard, reclining in my new chair with the heating pad on. At the peak of my relaxation, Phil came racing into the house, zoomed around the living room and my chair a couple of times, and shot like a cannon ball back outside. But he had grabbed something during his zooming and I hadn't gotten a good look. I soon realized he had grabbed one of my slippers and now was outside with it.

Aww CRAP!

I quickly un-reclined and un-relaxed and ran

outside, after grabbing my sloggers from the laundry room, to rescue my slipper from impending doom and Phil!

As I tugged on my sloggers, I saw Phil out behind the chicken shed trying to bury my slipper in the leaves.

"Phil, come here Phil!"

He looked up at me but continued digging. The slipper on the ground right in front of him.

"Phil! No, Phil!"

He ignored me.

"Aw, come on, Phil!"

He dug even more furiously, his giant paws raking the dirt and leaves.

I tugged on my boots and trip-walked at the same time, gaining ground on Phil and my doomed slipper. Phil saw me rapidly approaching, snatched up the slipper, and high-tailed it farther into the way-back forty.

I'm running and yelling, "Gawdammit, Phil!"

He gained a fair distance and tried once again to bury the slipper in the leaves under some brush. The slipper was on the ground next to him.

"PHIL!" I called.

I was hot on his tail but once again he grabbed the slipper and skipped-ran with it, feet beating ground, ears flapping away and a mile-wide grin on his face, all the while gripping the slipper in his teeth!

"Phil, you dirty dog...gimme my slipper! Stop, Phil, stop!"

He had made it to the way-back-forty fence by then. His giant paws raked the leaves, trying to find that perfect burial spot. The slipper remained in his grip. He kept glancing back and saw that I had gained ground. But I was not close enough to retrieve the slipper but close enough that he darted back around under the fallen tree bridge and headed for another burial site, slipper still in his toothly clutches.

"PHIL, PHIL!"

I backtracked around the fallen tree bridge and soon caught up with Phil, but again was not quite close enough to grab him or my slipper.

"Phil, you're killing me, buddy."

He ran through the brush, over the stumps and fallen limbs, leaped over large boulders.

"PHIL!"

And I did the same thing, in my pajamas, with my pink robe flapping behind me and wearing my sloggers.

"PHIL!"

Through the brush, through the brambles. Over hill. Over dale. Good gawd all mighty!

"Phil! Stop. Phil!"

This little guy was relentless.

Finally, as I rounded the remains of the exploded tree and after having traipsed all over the whole fuckin' way-back forty, I saw him sitting at the base of his favorite tree, the slipper on the ground right in front of him. Not in his teeth. And he wasn't digging.

"Good boy, Phil. Good boy."

He had finally given up trying to bury my slipper, and he let me come in and fetch it.

That night, my husband dropped one of his shoes and Phil was right there to grab it and run. I told Jeff not to worry—he eventually brings his toys back.

But Phil didn't make Daddy chase him. Not this time!

# HE'S A BIG BOY NOW

After having observed Phil in the backyard
for several weeks, I noticed he wouldn't
even try to escape through the fence. So,
I decided it was about time to remove the
jacket and outfit him with a proper grown-
up dog collar. I removed the GPS unit from
his jacket and attached it to his brand-new
collar, slipped it around his neck and sent
him on his way.

He paused for a hot minute before going out
the door. Like he was waiting for his jacket
to be put on. I gave him some praise and a
hug and told him it was okay, that the world
was his dog bone and go get 'em.

He passed a real good test that afternoon

when the neighbor's dog was loose. Phil barked at it through the fence along with our other dogs, but he stayed inside the fence.

He was a happy, contented dog all that day and for many days after!

# WHERE IS YOUR COLLAR?

One day, I was over at Gramma's when
I noticed Phil sitting on her front porch
without his collar.

"Oh great, Phil! Where is your new collar?"
*Oh, not to worry,* I immediately thought to
myself. I pulled out my phone and, using the
GPS locater app, located his collar. It was found
hung up on the fence in the way-back forty part
of the yard. Apparently, he had tried very hard
to get at something on the other side of the
fence and gotten his collar stuck. But he was
able to wriggle out of it. After retrieving Phil's
new collar, I clipped it back on him and set him
loose once again. The collar wouldn't be lost
again for a long time to come.

That GPS tracker was quite the tool!

# OUT AND ABOUT

 I was out and about with Phil one morning—in our yard, of course—playing, chasing and gathering toys. One of the toys was his special stuffed pig. He kept trying to convince me that pigs, even stuffed pigs, were outside pets. But I just wouldn't listen. That particularly special pig came in every night and rested on the third shelf of the bookcase so Phil could fetch it when he wanted it. He would take it back outside again in the mornings.

He has yet to
bury his special
stuffed pig.

However,
he snuck his
stuffed pet
duck outside
several weeks

ago and we've yet to find it. There were
several more inside toys that he managed
to drag outside and bury that would not
reappear for several weeks, if at all.

# DOGS ARE, CAN, AND WILL BE ICKY

With all his cuteness and exuberant personality, Phil, like a typical icky dog, picked up something from the grass, put it back down, rolled on it, picked it back up, rolled it around in his mouth for a hot sec, and spat it back out. And rolled on it again. I didn't know what it was. I really didn't want to get a closer look. But then Trudy, the really old bitch, strolled over and picked it up and carried it off somewhere out yonder. I saw her roll over on it too.

Some things, I just do not want to know what they are.

# NATE GOT PHIL'D!

Our young yard man we hired for the summer, Nate, had brought an extra pair of shoes with him one day when he showed up for work. He placed his phone on the patio table and dropped his shoes on the patio. Just dropped them on the patio!

Well, Jeff and I knew that you did not leave shoes on the ground. You do and you will fall victim to Phil.

*See the Slipper Incident for a little more clarification.*

Phil wasted no time at all and snatched up Nate's shoes, one at a time and ran off to hide them in a myriad of places around the backyard.

Poor Nate only noticed his shoes missing after he saw Phil run off with a rope toy and the kid went after him to fetch it. It was then that Nate was drawn to his shoe in the brush. However, he found only the one shoe. Phil was busted and he knew it. Phil trotted back to the patio and sat right next to Daddy like he was all innocent and everything.

I giggled about that for a long time after.

Later, Nate asked me if I knew of Phil's favorite hiding places.

"Yes," I said, and swept my arm to show the entire backyard.

Jeff decided to help the kid out so he rode around the two acres on his tractor to see if could spot the second shoe, but no luck. Phil did a good job hiding that one.

I told Nate, "Not to worry. It'll show up eventually".

Right before he was to take off for the day, Nate found his missing sneaker. Phil had it buried deep within the exploded tree.

Nate didn't leave his shoes on the ground after that.

# DADDY GOT PHIL'D. AGAIN!

One morning, Jeff was sitting outside on the back patio drinking his morning coffee when he looked out and noticed one of his work boots lying on the lawn.

"What the hell?" he said.

I would have loved to have seen how Phil had gotten that man's size thirteen, steel-toed work boot through the doggy door. Phil was quite determined when he puts his mind to it.

Jeff said, "Why now? They've been there forever and he's decided he wants to take them now?"

"Well," I said, "he believes he's stronger

now. Perhaps it's time you learn to put away

your shoes and boots."

Jeff is still learning, but occasionally
forgets and leaves his shoes on the floor and
Phil will sneak one out for good measure.

# THE BUGS OF AUGUST

## (my own personal experience with the bugs of Missouri)

Sooooo, the other day without thinking about it, I strolled out to the barn to see what was going on out there. Not once did I think about lawn bugs. Never fuckin' mind that every stinkin' bug in my backyard thinks I'm its food source. Never fuckin' mind that I had not bathed in Deep Woods OFF that day. Never fuckin' mind I knew for a fact there was a bug party going on in my grass because you could see them all jumping for joy every fuckin' time someone walked through it.

Sooooo, as I'm strolling mindlessly, every fuckin' party bug flew up my very loose, wide-legged pants and commenced to party the fuck away and gnaw on my nether regions like it was a fuckin' smorgasbord. These weren't chiggers, but they might as well have been. I swore that more than a few of those party bugs went back for seconds.

Imagine a bug rave going on in your pants. Complete with a DJ and strobe lights, glow-in-the-dark what-have-yous, and every-fuckin'-else that goes on at a rave.

I was chewed up from my knees to my waist and every-fuckin'-place in between. Seriously, e v e r y f u c k i n' p l a c e!

For just a brief moment I really felt sorry for the dogs. Especially the ones whose bellies were closest to the grass. Poor bastards!

Sooooo, I tried every bug bite potion there was. All of it. None of it helped. I bathed in the stuff. I just wanted to rip the skin off my body. My nether region hadn't felt that much action in I don't know how long.

I couldn't go outside, let alone go out in public, because I couldn't keep from scratching those fuckin bug bites. I looked like a damn pervert walking around with my hands in my pockets—or better yet—my arms inside my bibs just scratchin' away.

Sooooo, I was standing in the living room that night, fiercely scratching away and Jeff said, "I'm waiting for Brutus to yell at you to stop scratching yourself."

# BEAUTY TIP:

To keep the nose supple and soft apply a

daily mud pack!

# A VISIT FROM THE GROOMER

I called my regular groomer one day to inquire if she made house calls, specifically for trimming the dogs' nails. The seniors were hard to transport and the trauma of being in a salon for several hours was hard on them.

She said absolutely, she would be more than happy to come over.

She charged ten dollars a dog to trim their nails and she even put us on a regular schedule to stay on top of it.

Of course, all of the dogs were curious about that person and what she was doing to them. Each dog behaved relatively well. Only a couple put up a little resistance. There would be no snarling nor biting.

Phannie would go first, followed by Phred, then Phil. He was the least happy about the whole thing, reluctant but compliant nonetheless. When it was Brutus' turn, Phil was right there the whole time his nails were being clipped, up close and personal, intently watching the whole procedure, cocking his head right, then left, his brow crunched up like he was concentrating. As if some day he'd be clipping dogs' nails and he wanted to make sure he knew what he was doing.

# TOYS! MORE TOYS!

Phil was about two years old and very much enjoyed his toys.

 He got lots of toys. Because, you know, he was still a puppy and puppies enjoy their toys and he was spoiled.

Phil had his favorites, as most juvenile dogs did, and he protected those faves with all his might.

When he approached his toy cubby—i.e., the bookcase and all its shelves—he would eye it up and down until something caught his attention, at which time he would grab it off the shelf and do one of two things:

One—He would lay on the rug and chew on the chosen toy. Eventually, he would fall asleep for his mid-morning, midday, or mid-afternoon nap. They all took a lot of naps.

or...

Two—He would grab it firmly in his jaws and sprint out the back door to place it somewhere in the yard he thought would be appropriate. Usually, where he placed it depended on whether or not one of us was chasing after him to retrieve it, at which time Phil would carry said toy farther into the depths of the backyard. If we didn't chase after him, he would drop the toy on the patio and leave it.

Phil had toys that clearly belonged outside. There were tug ropes and quite a few toys that had been buried and dug up or chewed and torn beyond recognition. A couple of his toys had been buried in deer poop and obviously DID. NOT. BELONG. IN. THE. HOUSE!

Those really nasty, stinky toys ended up being thrown out.

Phil had toys that we tried to keep in the house so they would be available to bring him joy for a longer period of time. Those were the toys that Phil tried to take outside to hide and bury just to be ornery.

Sometimes, Phil succeeded in hiding a house toy so well that we couldn't find it.  More than once, his toy duck went missing for more than a month. When it did, we knew we weren't going to find it anytime soon. We had stopped looking for it. There were lots of places Phil would bury and hide his toys.

LOTS OF PLACES!

The toy duck made occasional appearances only to be hidden in another place very soon after. It remained an outside toy from then on.

One time, Phil went to the bookcase to fetch a toy and there weren't any. Oh no! No toys for Phil. He was so dismayed, he hung his

head and moped his way to the parlor and jumped on the couch and went to sleep. Without a toy.

Daddy had been lazy that day and forgot to bring in the toys. Bad Daddy!

Phil would carry all his toys and tubes through the dog door. He managed to get a man's boot, a cardboard box, even bath towels through that door.

He tried dragging Brutus through the dog door, but it wasn't big enough for the two of them.

# PAPER TOWEL TUBES

Paper towel tubes were among Phil's favorite toys. He would choose a paper towel tube over anything else, except maybe bacon or a cheeseburger. He would spend hours chewing on the tubes. He didn't eat it, just chewed on the fiber like gum. He would roll it around in his mouth, chew, roll it around and would spit out a wad of wet, chewed-up cardboard.

Those were always lovely to step on with bare feet.

His next favorite toys were his stuffed pigs. We tried to keep those inside but more often than not, Phil would haul them outside.

# LOOKING FOR A GHOST

On a typical fall day when the trees were gettin' nekkid, the air was crisp, the sky was cloudy, breezes blowing here and there, and it was cold enough you could feel your nipples harden underneath layers of shirts.

There was a caravan of people that showed up at the squatter house across the street to start clearing and cleaning it to get it ready to be put on the market. They brought with them their three dogs. Well, that got Phil's, Phred's, and Brutus' attention and the barking ensued.

Bark, bark, bark bark bark, fuckin bark bark bark, howl, howl, whimper, bark—you catch my drift. I would holler at Phil to stop barking and he would, for a minute, then he would start right up again. My solution, finally, was to load my pockets with doggie treats and distract the dogs. It worked.

I strolled out to the front fence to get their attention and had all four of them paying attention to me now. They all approached me, sat and each got a treat and off we went for a walk around the backyard. I had on my sloggers and my mission was to find the ghost chew toy Phil had hauled out of the house earlier that morning. The damn thing was bright white and about 10"x8" in size. You would have thought it would be easy to find in the fall leaves.

Noooooooooooooooooooooo! The turd-bucket

Phil was getting good at hiding his toys.

However, earlier that day, Daddy had gone

out exploring trying to find the ghost and had

returned with the duck that had been missing

for the last several months. So you never knew.

Phred, old and gimpy; Phannie, extra old

and super gimpy; and Phil, young and fit as a

fiddle, stayed with me the whole trip around

the way-back forty. About halfway around

Brutus was like *'Fuck this noise. It's cold out*

*here and I'm going in where it's warm. You*

*can keep your stoopid snacks.'*

Phred, Brutus, Phannie and Phil and I had

a good time crunching through the fallen

leaves. But, alas, we wouldn't find the ghost

chew toy.

## THE GHOST WAS FOUND. HOWEVER...

On an early fall morning, Phil hauled out

a hard-rubber chew toy in the shape of

a robot. The damn thing weighed about a

pound. And if left in the middle of the floor

was a serious toe stumper. Usually, he would

 haul it to the

patio and drop

it. Sometimes he

brought it back in

the house to chew

on. That day though he grabbed that robot

by the arm and hauled it through the doggy

door and continued right off the patio, down

the side of Mom's house, headed toward the

barn and beyond. That particular toy was

not so easy to spot as it was dark blue and gray. If the yard boy hit that thing with the mower, it was gonna make a helluva racket and probably bend a blade.

Daddy had gone out back to see if he could locate the hard-rubber chew toy robot. He wasn't able to traverse the way-back forty without great difficulty, so he pretty much stuck to front of the barn and the exploded tree. He was out there for a good thirty minutes or so.  When he came gimping back, I was damned to see that he had the bright-white ghost, which wasn't so bright white, in his grasp. He had found it by the exploded-tree fire pit which showed us that Phil had and still continued to relocate his toys around the yard.

Certain toys, whether they were stuffies or chewies, started out as house toys. But after having been outside, hidden within and around all the crevices and cracks and weeds and leaves and critter tunnels of the way-back forty, they eventually became outside toys on a full-time basis.

Duck and Ghost were then considered outside toys. FULL TIME!

The robot was not to be located. I hoped we would find it before the boy came to compost-mow the backyard.

(The robot was never found)

# PHIL'S ANNUAL CHECKUP

Phil and Brutus had vet appointments for their annual vaccinations. It was hard to believe a year had passed. And so quickly.

I proceeded to load Phil and Brutus into the back seat of the Kia. Brutus went right in, and I thought maybe Phil would follow. Phil DID NOT, WOULD NOT, and flat out REFUSED to get in the car. I had to pick up the little fat fuck and put him on the seat. He was not happy with Mommy. And I was not happy with him—the little shit weighed a ton.

I got to the vet's office. Managed to wrangle the dogs inside and then the real fun began.

Brutus, at this time, was only interested in going back to the car and had his forehead pressed firmly against the glass door, would only weigh himself if I got on the scales first. At first, he got just two legs on the scale. With a little coaxing, I got him to get all four on the scale, then somehow kept him there while I quickly stepped off. Finally, Brutus weighed in at his normal fifty-four pounds.

So it was the little fat fuck's turn. Phil sat down on the floor at first. Then he laid down and immediately willed himself to be a hundred pounds of clay. Seriously, how the hell do they do that?

Phil was like, "No fuckin' way am I getting on that scale!"

I groaned out loud while trying to conjure up the muscles needed to pick him up and place him on the scale. He weighed in at forty pounds. And, no I wasn't stepping on the scale!

"HOLYYYYYY SHITTTTT!"

In the meantime Kim, the receptionist, was cracking up behind the desk, and fell out of her chair over my handling of fat fuck Phil. Glad I could provide a little comic relief to your day, Kim.

So, I led the doggos into the exam room and I finally sat down and caught my breath. The doc came in and said, "We'll get Phil first,"

And proceeded to bend down and pick him up.

"OOMPHH!" the vet exclaimed at having to hoist fat Phil onto the table.

The vet told me what I already knew needed to happen. Phil had to go on a major diet to lose five pounds in one month. Then five more pounds the next month.

"Ain't this gonna be fun!"

When it was all said and done and I'd depleted my checking account, I asked Dr. Boschen if he would help me load Phil back in the car. And he did. I love this vet in all ways.

Phil pulled the one-hundred-pound trick again by immediately laying on the ground. Thankfully, Dr. Boschen was strong and capable and was able to load the dog in the car.

I had a feeling Phil would not be a car-ride kind of dog.

# ONE MONTH WEIGH-IN DAY

Today marked one month since Phil was put on a diet. His—I mean *our*—mission was for him to lose five pounds in one month. The vet rationed him to 1/4 cup of kibble twice a day and nothing else. Which looked just like twelve pieces when in his bowl. Damn!

We tried, we really did. His food was rationed, snacks were virtually eliminated, and short of raking the two acres to get rid of the acorns and deer poop, we did pretty well. The squirrels had some serious competition for the acorns during this time.

I mean this poor dude, for the last couple of days, was aggressively infringing on the other dogs' food. Didn't turn out too well in a couple instances, but no blood was shed, so I guess that's a good thing.

Maybe!

So, this morning was the day to take poor fat Phil to the vet's office to be weighed. No appointment necessary, just a weigh and a notation on his chart. No problem. Easy peasy, right?

Fuck! I get the leash on him, open the gate to go out and he would not go through the gate. He absofuckinlutely refused to walk through that gate. I even tried treats. As soon as we approached the gate, he would back up. He once backed right out of his collar.

Okay, fine, you big fat turd bucket! We'll try

the front door then. *Nope! Nada! No bueno!* He was having nothing to do with any of it.

Well, I guess the next best thing was to pick his fat ass up. So I got him on the couch, hoisted his ass into my arms and proceeded to haul his fat ass out to the car.

Into the back seat he went and off to the vet's we went.

We arrived. He jumped out of the car, no problem, and proceeded to pee on each of the posts outside the door. But he balked crossing the threshold, so I bent down and gave his ass a shove and in we went.

Yay, I got him in the lobby. The next step was to get his ass on the scale so we could figure out if this diet thing was working.

Phil would not have anything to do with anything at this point and was working extra hard at not cooperating.

"Bullshit, you little fat fuck!" I called out. Kim, the receptionist, was having a good laugh at our expense. So I exerted control and picked up his fat ass, again, and placed him on the scale, all four feet too. He was pissed and immediately folded his legs under himself, like little hydraulic limbs, and laid on the scale. Now when he pulled his obstinate character, he would make himself seem heavier, so really not helping his cause.

He weighed in at an even forty-two pounds! He had lost 3.6 pounds. We didn't quite reach his goal, but we're a work in progress as he did appear to have a little thinner ass!

Or so Kim, the vet's assistant, said.

So, out we go, Phil following obediently (finally), but again, although he didn't lay on the ground, I still had to lift him up to put him in the car. We then headed home. Once there he avoided me for a good two hours.

We would continue to work on his diet and I, for one, would be happier when he lost a few more pounds. He wouldn't be so heavy to lift.

# SO DONE WITH THIS FUCKIN' DIET!

Phil was so done with his diet. He was getting aggressive, trying to steal the other dogs' dinners. He scarfed his food down so goddamn fast I doubt he was even tasting it.

I had to stand between him and Phannie until she was done. Then I had to stand between him and Brutus, because Brutus had manners and didn't scarf his food like it was a rare steak! There were a couple of instances where I had to grab Phil by the collar and hold him back to keep him from getting his face ripped off by Trudy, the genuinely old matriarch of the bunch. Thankfully, no persons nor dogs were injured, but it still made me take a step back.

I decided that Phil was looking positively good, having lost close to five pounds, so I started feeding him a maintenance diet. I wouldn't traumatize the guy with any more trips to the vet. Not until the following year!

To me, Phil was a perfectly fine specimen of a short-legged, long-eared, stocky-bodied beagle with huge feet and I loved him crazily, even though he ate one of my bras and Daddy's shoes.

I have heard that dogs choose their
people. I believe it!

# WE SAVED A LIFE

The sun had finally come through on a crisp
fall morning. Phil was dancing, then sitting
and barking at a section of fence toward the
back forty by the empty lot next door. He
would bark, bark, barkbarkbark, howllll, bark
some more then sit a spell.  He repeated his
barking-sitting-barking for several minutes.
He was obviously transfixed and excited and
concerned all at the same time.

I had been standing on the patio drinking my
morning coffee listening and watching and
it started to sound like Phil was in distress.
I hurried back into the house to get my
sloggers on and grab a coat. I walked rapidly
out to where Phil was still barking and

hollering. I got closer and looked over the fence. My first thought was, *what the hell am I looking at?*

It was a fuckin' possum with its stupid head stuck in a glass mason jar.

Yep, you read that right. A possum had its head stuck in a jar.

Yeah, you just don't see that every day. You might have read about it. You might have even seen it on YouTube. But who has actually ever seen a real live possum with its head stuck in a fuckin' mason jar?

I had to do something, so I walked back into the house and dialed up animal control. They're never open when you need them.

*Christ, now what? I'm not going to climb over*

*the fence and pluck a possum out of a jar.*
*I'm not touching it. NO WAY JOSE!*

The other alternative I could think of was
to call the sheriff's office. We've called
them before with wild or stray animal issues.
So I called. A few minutes later, a young
deputy showed up. I'm just gonna say this....
boyoboyoman, that deputy was FINE! Tall,
dark and very handsome. He obviously worked
out because he filled out his uniform quite
nicely. It made my day when he showed up.

I happily walked the deputy back to the
spot where the stupid possum was laying
on a log with its head stuck in a jar. The
deputy checked out the situation, decided
he needed a couple of things and headed

back to his patrol car. I went back inside the house to retrieve the step stool because he would need it to get over the fence.

The deputy returned and we continued to walk toward the stupid possum with a jar stuck on its head, and me carrying the step stool.

The deputy found a strong post with a good spot in the fence to climb over. I was very tempted to help steady him by placing my hands on his butt, but it was just a fleeting thought. I didn't want to get arrested for assault. So, I kept my hands to myself. He gloved up, grabbed the jar from the bottom with the possum dangling by its head, gave it three good shakes and POP went the possum's head. It literally made a POP. The semi-stunned possum shook his head a few times and scrambled back into the woods without looking back. Ingrate!

I thanked the deputy and threw away the mason jar.

I was grateful that the possum's head popped out of the jar. The only other alternative would have been to shoot it. The deputy didn't want to resort to that and I, without a doubt, was not going to stick around for that.

That day we saved a life, and that stupid possum no doubt returned to tease Phil, and hopefully, he kept his head out of glass mason jars.

# WE SAID GOODBYE TO PHRED

With a very heavy heart we had prepared our beloved Phred for her journey across the rainbow bridge. Phred had been one of us for about fifteen years. She had come to us as a one-year-old stray joining the pack of dogs we already had at the time.

Phred was your typical lab. Smart, curious, funny, faithful and super sweet.

Over the last couple of years, Phred's health had started to decline. She had developed epilepsy that resulted in seizures that increased in severity over a short time, even though she had been on medication. A couple of the seizures resulted in muscle damage to her hind legs, which caused her to have trouble standing and remaining standing. Her medications had her panting heavily and the drool was insane. She was in so much discomfort she whined most of her waking hours. There would be no more comforting her. She was beyond that.

It was time that Daddy and I had a long and very tearful conversation about Phred's end of life. It would be a tough, gut-wrenching call to make.

We decided to set aside our own selfishness because Phred didn't deserve to suffer any longer. She had had enough.

We made the appointment with the vet for the following morning.

We said our final goodbyes and she was gone.

Phred would be the second dog we lost that year and the first of three we would lose that month.

# HERE COMES TROUBLE

One afternoon, Phil came plodding into the living room from the kitchen. As he entered the living room, I said out loud to Daddy, "Look, there's trouble."

Phil stopped in his tracks and turned his head to look behind himself.

# BUCKETS OF RAIN FORCE A CHANGE

One of the endearing things Phil did was grab a toy from the toy bin following a nap. It usually didn't matter which. He would then dash out the dog door, carrying the toy to the backyard, where he would deposit it under the clothesline about ten feet west of the uncovered part of the patio. If we chased after him, he would grab the toy and dash out toward the barn. Sometimes beyond.

Phil would always greet us at the gate and even with a toy in his mouth, he would make all kinds of beagle noises, and his body would be all wiggly-waggly. If he liked you when he met you for the first time, he would greet you with a toy and body wiggles. Sometimes he would even present you with a leaf.

It was one of his most endearing traits.

Every so often, he brought an outside toy into the house. Inside toys were inside toys until they became too grody and mangled and were then relegated to outside toys.

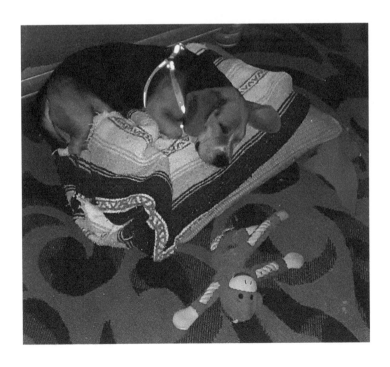

One particularly nasty, cold, wet, windy day, right before dinner, the doggos were waking up from their early afternoon naps. Phil grabbed a fat stuffed snowman from his toy bin and dashed out the dog door. I couldn't catch him in time, but I nonetheless rushed to the back door. I stood there and watched as he stood at the edge of the patio under the patio roof, looking out at the sheets of rain. Phil seemed to have a change of mind and he came back toward the door. As he got closer, though, he pivoted right and scampered to the opposite edge of the patio. The edge that had no covering. He skidded to a stop at the sight of the buckets of rain coming down. I had just turned around for a second to come back inside and here came Phil skipping toward me with the stuffed snowman still in his mouth. He brought it back into the house via the dog door, continued through the kitchen, and deposited it back on the pile of dog toys.

He then made himself comfortable on his favorite chair.

# NOT JUST ANOTHER DOG...

Brutus had not been eating right his last week and he had lost a lot of weight and had gotten visibly boney.

He wasn't the normal, laid back, could-give-two-fucks-about-anything Brutus. He had become exceptionally clingy, reacting slower to any stimulation and had so little energy. So I dialed Dr. Boschen and was able to get him in to the vet that morning.

Doctor Boschen checked him out and remarked that Brutus' stomach felt distended and he wanted to get an x-ray of his abdomen. He said to leave Brutus there and they would call me in an hour or so to let me know when it was good to come for him.

When I got home, I did some research about  distended stomachs in dogs and it wasn't good news. It was the worst news. The tears were welling up already.

"Shit, shit, shit."

The vet called. It was time to come back. We showed up, masked because of the pandemic, and followed the doctor to the back room where Brutus would be waiting for us. The doctor went on to explain that they found a tumor about the size of a cantaloupe that would be inoperable. Brutus wouldn't have had more than a few days left to live and the suffering would be awful. He had lost ten pounds in that last couple

months and it would have only gotten worse for him. Any food I fed him was just feeding the tumor.

We made the heart-wrenching decision to end his life before the suffering got worse.

I spent the next hour saying goodbye to my sweet boy. I scratched his boney head and gave him big mama dog type of hugs and told him that he was the bestest boy ever and he was going to be okay. I removed his collar, put it in my pocket and I hugged him again and told him he was a good boy one last time before we left the office.

Brutus was about twelve and lived with us for almost ten years. He was my first male dog. He was *'my boy'* as much as Phil was *'my boy'* too. Brutus was an exceptionally good-natured dog. Not a particularly cuddly type of dog but was rather satisfied with a head scratch and a pat on the butt. Although, he did enjoy a good mama dog kind of hug. He would come up to me and place his chin on my lap and that would be his signal he wanted a hug. And he would hug back.

I still miss my boy!

# THEY WERE ALL JUST SO OLD

I have been a dog mom for about eighteen years. Every dog we had we rescued off the streets, literally! They were all strays we took in and made part of our family. Most of them were pups, not more than a year or eighteen months old at the time. That was such a long time ago.

That year had been a rough one because our doggos were leaving us for their journeys across the so-called rainbow bridge to doggy heaven. Phoebe, Phred, then Brutus! It was a brutal time. We still had two genuinely old bitches hanging on by a thread, Trudy and Phannie. They could barely stand up on their own and both were on pain meds for old dog issues like arthritis. And Phannie had developed congestive heart and incontinence issues.

Shortly after Brutus passed, Phannie lost her life to old age. As with all the others, she too was a particularly good-natured dog. Phannie was a typical Beagle in how she found ways to escape but always, always

 came right back home. She was a funny and faithful little dog!

I miss her ornerynous.

# AND THEN THERE WAS PHRANCIS

Shortly after Brutus passed away, I noticed
Phil moping about, being all sad and lonely

 and he seemed
depressed. I decided
to look for him a new
companion dog. His
very own puppy. It
took about a week,
and we found this

beautiful nine-month-old red heeler. We

named her Phrancis.

The first couple of days were quite hectic.
Phrancis was learning her place in the
hierarchy and fending off Phil's advances

at the same time. She had just been spayed and still had pheromones that Phil would not, could not, absofuckinlutely refused to ignore.

By the second day, Phrancis had pretty much let the horny dude know that his constant humping, whether it was on her or near her, was not—repeat—NOT going to be tolerated. They literally tussled and rolled around with their legs wrapped around each other like professional wrestlers and would carry on like that for a good twenty minutes until they pooped each other out. She met his every attempt with the same move until he finally figured out that he had met his match and resolved to put an end to his humping. Or perhaps he got tired of getting sprayed with water by me every time he attempted to mount her. Either way, it had not taken too long for him to unmaster the hump. Smart puppies!

By day three, the doggos started to settle down a little. Phil had pretty much given up on humping Phrancis at every turn. It was a good thing too. Phil had started humping air just being next to her. I was afraid he would give himself a hernia. And it was embarrassing!

The next priority would be the teeth and biting. Yesterday, they were going at it with their mouths wide open and fangs out. You could actually hear the teeth clacking against each other. We were still working

on the biting.
Phrancis would
get jelly and
used her teeth
to grab my
arm and pull
my hand away
from Phil when
I would pet
him. Phrancis did not know her own strength.
So, for Phrancis there were lots of 'easy
girl' and with only a couple sprays from the
bottle, it started to get better. We still had
work to do.

Phil was being the bestest, goodest boy ever
where his toys were concerned. He had no
problem sharing his toys and he even showed

Phrancis how to dash out the doggy door with one his grip. At the end of the day, there were toys spread from room to room to room and I loved every bit of it.

Phrancis bonded with me easily and followed me everywhere, always keeping me in her sights. She learned to like Phil and would shadow him outside whilst he showed her the ropes, like the fence line patrol patterns, where the ugliest toys got buried, and where to look for fresh deer poop. I think he lost two pounds in those first days.

It would continue to go well.

# THE GREAT ESCAPE

We had finally reached snow-melting temperatures.

That afternoon, Phil and Phrancis were in the yard playing at the base of a large tree. They were standing side-by-side, tails held up high and wagging, and their heads buried in the snowbank, popping up every few seconds, only to shove them back in again. They had something! They moved in unison around that tree, side-stepping, snouting, side-step, snout some more. Around the tree they went. Suddenly, something popped out of the snow, about the size of a small dirt clod, and as quickly as it popped up it dove back down into the snowbank. Phrancis saw it first and pounced. It popped up again! This time, Phil saw it and pounced. I was watching a dog's version of whack a mole! As Phil and Phrancis pounced, dug and shoved their faces into the snowbank at the base of the tree, the little brown dirt clod popped up out of the snow again, but behind the dogs. Those mutts were pouncing and snouting and did not even notice the little brown dirt clod as it quietly burst out of the snow and ran like its little life depended on it, which of course it did. It had about ten yards to go to make it to life, liberty, and justice for all. That little brown dirt clod scurried on top of the snow, plowed through the snowbank at the garden fence, only five more yards to go and it's bounding in and out of the snowbanks, stealthily and without haste making its way to the fence to freedom. Little brown dirt clod made it out alive, and the two mutts didn't have a clue.

After a few more minutes of snuffling, digging and pushing through the snow, Phil finally nosed out the track the little brown dirt clod had made in the snow and snuffled it all the way to the fence where little brown dirt clod had escaped through with its life.

Little brown dirt clod (mole)-1...Phil and Phrancis-0

In life, going up is just as it is coming down - sideways and one foot at a time!

# A WALK IN THE WOODS

Finally, we had beautiful weather. It was dry, breezy, a cool fifty degrees. The snow had finally dissipated, and the ground was relatively dry. It would be a good day to take a hike around the way-back forty of our yard.

I stepped into my sloggers, slipped on a jacket, grabbed my camera phone and headed out for a walk in the way-back forty woods.

It didn't take but a few seconds for Phil and Phrancis to hear me and come a-charging. They walked with me for about a New York minute and got quickly distracted by something moving in the brush. I felt sorry for the 'somethings moving in the brush' with these two dogs around.

As I neared the back fenceline I was
stunned to see that the property directly
behind us on the other side of our fence
had been cleared and cleaned up. It had
been such an eyesore before—nasty, giant
trash heaps, building debris and overgrown
everything. To see it cleaned up and cleared
of piles of trash, torn-down structures, and
other construction debris almost brought me
to my knees in astonishment.

*DAMN—our property value just went up*
*$10K!*

Once I regained my composure I carried on.

I managed to gather up a few dog toys
that had been lost, deposited, or otherwise
discarded in the woods on my way through

the way-back forty. My jacket pockets became full.

Phil and Phrancis ran around with their noses to the ground, searching for the next 'something in the brush' to chase or better yet to roll in. Sometimes they chased after thrown toys and occasionally brought them back to me.

I was so enthralled by the cleaned-up woods behind us that I forgot I had my camera on me.

That day, I rescued six toys and found only two pieces of garbage on my walk. I thoroughly enjoyed the company of both doggos and the sunshine felt good on our souls.

# TEAMWORK MAKES THE DREAM WORK.

The weather was behaving like early spring weather should behave. It was warm and breezy. Trees were budding and tulips and daffies were peeking through the winter ground. It was all so refreshing. Even the air smelled good.

I was hanging some bedding on the clothesline for airing out. As I wrestled the bedspread over the line, about the only kind of wrestling I engaged in anymore, I noticed the dogs were busy with their own kind of airing out.

Phil, Phrancis, and even ancient-old bitch Trudy had their collected and undivided attention on a mound of dirt and rock and weeds and other things growing and dying on a berm next to the century oak and about five yards from the clothesline where I was working.

Trudy stood on the mound, looking like the retired acting-supervisor. She just stood back and oversaw the two youngsters and assessed their digging skills. She was way beyond doing any actual digging herself. My gawd, she was a hundred-thirty years old! She could barely stand up straight. So rightfully, she shouldn't have been doing any digging. But she still had the will to stand there and observe. More often than not getting sprayed with dirt.

Phil and Phrancis could not have given two flicks of the tail about what old bitch Trudy was or wasn't doing or what she was or wasn't thinking. They flung dirt on her like she wasn't even there. They almost seemed to be enjoying themselves. Trudy did her best to stay out of the way, but the dirt found her wherever she stood.

Fuckin' kids!

Phil and Phrancis were fanatically taking turns inserting their heads into the hole they had dug. The one with their head in the hole would dig, dig, diggidydigdig, displacing dirt in every direction, and always flinging some on Trudy, whilst the one with their head above ground kept watch to make sure nothing escaped, if in fact something actually tried to make a run for it. It's happened before. They had learned their lesson.

And we all knew Trudy wouldn't be able to catch a snail if one were to crawl past, let alone any four-legged critter running for its life. But at least she had the will to just stand there on that mound of dirt and look damn good doing it.

You don't see this kind of teamwork on any road crew!

In the end, their only takeaway was a piece of root.

# WHAT THEY DON'T KNOW...

I was outside on the back patio basking in
the sun. Phil was sitting next to me. After a

minute, he got
up and walked
away from me
toward the
backyard, with
his tail held
high and proud.

He had sat
on a cherry

blossom petal, and it was stuck, perfectly
centered on his asshole like a little pastie!

Spaghetti night
always drew
a crowd. (l-r:
Phred, Phil,
Brutus)

Phil was always
interested in
what I was
doing.

Looking East onto half of the backyard.

The Exploded
Tree where dog
toys went to die.

Phrancis being affectionate.

Chillin' on a sunny afternoon. (Phannie, Phil, Brutus, Phred)

# STAND-OFF OVER LEFTOVERS

Each of the dogs had their own chosen spot where to eat their food. Phrancis ate in the laundry room. Phil ate in the office. And Trudy ate in the kitchen. Each separated by a door for a more enjoyable meal experience.

Phil ate his kibble like the Cookie Monster ate his cookies. Grunting! Snorting! Numnumnummmmnum! Kibble flew in all directions. He ate his meals with gusto. And then there was the very loud and obnoxious belch after he was done.

Phrancis was a slightly milder version of the Cookie Monster. There was less grunting, and less kibble flew. But she too ate fast and she too belched when she was done.

Trudy, however, was a slow and deliberate eater. She would pick up a morsel, chew on it while making a right-hand stagger-step around her dish. She would then take another bite and stagger-stepped some more to the right.

She was old. Something like a hundred-thirty, maybe even older. It didn't matter; she was certainly entitled to stagger-step whenever and wherever she could. I hoped I could stagger-step that good when I got to be her age. Eventually, she would lay on her side with her front paws spread out and her plate placed between them. She seemed to be more comfortable eating that way.

As Trudy ate, it was not uncommon for her

to drop a few morsels on the rug. Ones that she really didn't feel like eating.

If she didn't like it. No problem. She just spat it out on the rug.

Sometimes she would finish up the dropped morsels. Other times not so much.

When she finished eating, morsels, of course, would be left on the rug. Trudy stagger-stepped her way into the living room, like she usually did when she was done, but that evening, she quickly about-faced and returned and stood over the morsels. She had no intention of eating those nasty morsels she had purposely spat out. Trudy was the reigning bitch; she knew it and she wanted everyone else to know it!

Phil and Phrancis were lying next to me in the office, knowing full well that if they got within two feet of Trudy and those morsels, she would eat their faces. She was of the mind that she could literally rip their faces right off. And she would not give two flips of her tail about it either!

She was a bitch like that.

She kept on teasing Phil and Phrancis. She wanted a fight. I was not sure where a hundred-thirty-year-old dog got the energy, but Trudy was in the mood.

She had gotten in the two youngsters' faces earlier in the day because they were playing, and she just was not having anymore of it. Poor Phrancis had shrunk away, her ears down and slinked behind me for protection. Apparently, she had had her face ripped off by Trudy earlier and I hadn't known about it. Phrancis had quickly learned that retreat would be her best choice for survival, with her face intact!

So, Phil and Phrancis sat patiently next to me and outwaited, or outwitted Trudy, who eventually gave up, walked away and didn't return.

I gave the two youngsters the go ahead and they leaped at the opportunity to nab a morsel and not get their faces ripped off.

# PHRANCIS AND THE TURTLE

I was sitting on the patio, enjoying the warmth of a spring sun when I heard yipping and barking out in the yard. I looked up and noticed Phrancis circling around something in the grass, occasionally lunging at it and yip-yapping.

I already had my sloggers on, so I strolled out to where the action was. Upon seeing my approach, Phrancis immediately sat and looked at me then at something in the grass, up at me again. I followed her gaze and found myself looking at a box turtle. It was box turtle migration time and our yard was their path to wherever the turtles went.

Apparently, it was the first turtle that

 Phrancis had ever seen.

I giggled out loud to myself and she looked up at me puzzled, her brow furrowed. I patted her on the head then reached down and touched the turtle. As I was petting the turtle, I said to Phrancis, "It's okay, it's just a turtle. It won't hurt you."

I'd pet the dog. Pet the turtle. Pet the dog. Pet the turtle. All the while repeating the phrase, "It's okay, it's just a turtle," to Phrancis. After a few minutes, she seemed to understand that the turtle wasn't a threat to her, or me or anyone or anything else for that matter and eventually walked away from it and left it alone for the rest of the day.

Pet the dog. Pet the turtle. Pet the dog. Pet the turtle.

# SO. MANY. HUMANS.

For the first couple years of Phil's residency with us and for the first few months of Phrancis', it was just we three humans and, besides themselves, a really old bitchy dog. That was it.

Three humans. Two and a half dogs. Two acres. Two houses. A barn. A run-down chicken shack. The perfect habitat. The perfect ambiance. Quiet. Serene. Birds. Squirrels. Turtles. A little slice of heaven if you would.

And then the family came to visit.

A whole lotta family! So many humans!

Our youngest daughter, Heather; her

partner in life, Matt; their three kids ranging in age from five to eighteen had flown out from Washington for a two-week visit. That Saturday, Heather's family along with her older sister, her sister's husband and their two young boys plus an aunt—all local yokals—descended on our home for a Father's Day/Birthday/Graduation party that would last an entire day.

Now the invasion of all of those humans didn't all happen all at once. The Washington folks would stop by for brief visits leading up to that day. But even with just a few humans at a time, Phil was just not happy having company over.

He hid behind a chair in the living room and

stayed there until company left. We tried coaxing him out with treats, and that was a no-go. Poor Matt did his best to get Phil to be comfortable with him. He was quite disappointed because having only met Phil online, and having a beagle of his own, he was really hoping to be best uncle to Phil.

Nope. Nada. Wasn't going to happen according to Phil. He already had a mama. A daddy. A gramma. He even had his own puppy, Phrancis. He didn't need no stinkin' uncle.

On the big day, the day an army of humans would descend on the dogs' home and yard and all it contained, Phil did everything he could to avoid the new company as best as he could. It wasn't easy to hide in a small house when it was full of humans running in and out and everywhere. Behind Mommy's chair seemed the best option and so that was where he stayed, with his head under the chair and his tail tucked safely out of the way. He had already mapped out his escape routes in case of invading humans, so he was as comfortable as he was going to get at that moment, and he slept the day away.

Phrancis was at first a little wary, but after a few minutes would relax herself and carefully approach everyone. She wasn't aggressive. She didn't jump on anyone. She was consciously being the very best version of herself.

There turned out to be one particularly small human Phrancis would attach herself to. He was five years old and a very shy and quiet little boy named Mo. She followed that little human  wherever he went and would ever so gently take his arm and lead him to places she wanted him to see. (She was a red heeler, after all, and that's what they did, herd and lead). I stayed close at all times because Phrancis used her mouth and teeth to lead and herd, but she had been a very gentle dog and never left a mark on anyone. I just wanted to make sure she was going to be extra gentle with that little boy. And she was. Very much so.

Little Mo liked to find a shady spot and sit in it and Phrancis would be right next to him. Both of them just chillin' in the shade on a hot summer day. Just a boy and his dog.

But Phil. He had nothing to do with any of it. Not even for a yummy treat. He stayed behind Mommy's chair until the coast was clear.

Then that big party day arrived. Saturday. A day that would be full of activity and humans. Humans everywhere. There would be fourteen humans in total. To Phil, I'm sure, it must have felt like he was in the big city for the first time and all the bustling of humans big and small was just too much stimulation and overwhelming as hell.

He was a shy little country dog getting caught up in big city shit and he wasn't happy or comfortable with any of it. He stayed behind Mommy's chair.

For the most part, the majority of activity occurred outside on the large patio and around the backyard. If there were humans in the house, they were in the kitchen and sometimes in the bathroom. But rarely humans in the living room where Mommy's chair was and where Phil decided he would be just fine right there. And if he kept his head under the chair, he wouldn't be able to see anyone, which in his mind meant they couldn't see him either.

So whilst Phil was hiding, Phrancis had immersed herself into the full experience of small, medium, and large humans who were eating and drinking and either on purpose or on accident, dropping morsels on the ground, which without hesitation she would swoop in and snatch up. One of the kids dropped a good-sized chunk of cake on the patio and before that kid said, "Ohhhhhh nooooo," Phrancis had that cake in her mouth. There would be no retrieval of that piece of cake!

There was so much food and I'm sure Phrancis had a taste of just about everything. She was spotted lapping up some root beer someone had spilled on the patio.

The party went on for several hours. And Phrancis would be right in the middle of it, all the while behaving very well. She didn't snatch any food from anyone's lap or plate, instead sat in front of them, hoping they were in a sharing mood. If they weren't, she would move on to the next person. Sitting, smiling, and hoping.

At some point in the afternoon, Phil decided he would check to see what was going on or not going on. He hadn't seen or heard anyone come through the living room in a while, so he just assumed the coast was clear.

He poked his head through his dog door, just his head, took a quick look around and saw humans. Lots of humans. Too many humans. So many humans he couldn't count them all.

Someone called his name.

An *oh-shit* look crossed his face and he

quickly retracted his head from the dog door, backed into the office and straight away returned to hiding behind Mommy's chair.

The coast was NOT clear! Damnit!

On the day the visitors from Washington returned home, Phil decided he would make friends with Matt.

When the kids stopped by the house on their way to the airport, Phil greeted Uncle Matt when he walked in the door with a very robust howl and body-wiggled his way over for a pet.

It so thrilled Uncle Matt that finally Phil had accepted him and they would become best long-distance buddies for a long time to come.

It took Phil several days to recover from all the fun and excitement that was a family reunion. I'm sure he suffered a minor bout of doggy PTSD; he startled so easily for those few days afterward.

It took several days for Phil to find his normal laid-back country dog self.

We prefer the quiet country life over the bustling city life any day.

# PHRANCIS VS. PIG

Phrancis became my constant buddy. She was my shadow. When I visited my mom, aka Gramma, Phrancis was at my side by the time I reached her front door, about fifteen feet away. On those early morning visits, Mom would sit up in her bed with her fresh cup of coffee and Phrancis and I would enter her house and room, me still in my robe also with a fresh cup of coffee in hand. Phrancis would leap up on the bed and lay next to Mom, but not before she sniffed out all the pillows and books that were on top of the bed. It would become our morning routine and the visits I enjoyed the most.

We made frequent visits to Mom's place. After all, she lived just fifteen feet behind us, across the back patio and up three steps to her front door. It was a ridiculously awesome arrangement for all of us.

One afternoon, Phrancis and I were visiting, seated in the living room. Nothing changed as far as furnishings were concerned or where they were placed in the whole time Mom lived there. When you came through the glass front door, there was a coatrack on your left, then a recliner chair; usually with the gramma in it. To the left of that, a loveseat and a table.

I'd sit on the couch, Gramma in her chair and Phrancis would settle down on the rug in front of the door.

One day, Gramma and I were chatting away

and Phrancis suddenly stood, all hackled from head to tail and growling at something in the corner where the coatrack stood.

She. Was. Serious.

I had not seen her like this before and it kind of freaked me out.

I stood up and walked toward her and looked at what I thought she was staring at. She continued to be all hackled up and growling and I tried to settle her down. I just couldn't see anything. I ruffled through the contents of a basket Gramma kept on the floor next to her chair, thinking there might have been a mouse in it. Nothing.

I patted the purse hanging on the coatrack. Nothing popped out.

Phrancis still growling.

"What the hell, girl?"

And then it dawned on me. She continued to stare at something on the floor. She was growling at the gawdamn ceramic pig that stood on the floor at the base of the coatrack. That stupid ceramic pig had been there for years. It never moved. And all of a sudden Phrancis felt threatened by it.

OMG! It's *the turtle incident* all over again.

In a soothing voice, void of laughter, maybe a few snickers, I tell Phrancis, "It's okay, Phrancis. It's okay, honey."

And I'm petting her as well, getting her hackles down, but not before I pet the pig.

Pet the pig. Pet the dog. Pet the pig.
Pet the dog.

After a few minutes of consoling her,
Phrancis settled back down on the mat and
all was good.

She would let no human, turtle, or pig bring
harm to her mama. She was that faithful and
protective.

No pig nor dog was harmed during that nor
any other visits to Gramma's.

# LIFE IS GOOD WHEN THERE ARE DOGS IN IT.

Both dogs brought their own kind of personalities, smarts and a sense of wonder to the family. Along with an endless supply of comic relief.

Phil had accepted Phrancis as his bestie and they were often seen together wherever they roamed about the yard. In the several months since Phrancis' arrival, he had lost a few more pounds and was looking downright buff. I didn't think it would be possible for him to get any handsomer.

He had escaped a couple more times through part of the fence that had been previously ziptied. Phrancis aided and abetted his

escapes by chewing through the zipties that

held the fence tight. It didn't take long

to apprehend his ass and bring him home

though. He had to wear the 'coat of shame'

for a day or two so we could find the breach

and fix it. It was a good thing we kept one

stashed away for such an occasion.

Trudy continued to intimidate Phrancis

just for the hell of it. She would slowly and

menacingly make her way toward Phrancis with a purposeful look and Phrancis would shrink away, her ears tucked straight back against her head. The funny thing was that this happened in the house only. Outside, Trudy didn't play any mind games with Phrancis at all. She would play games with the neighbor's dogs by instigating an

argument then standing back to watch. She was just a bitch like that.

Over the years, Phil had developed into a lovable, spirited

and loving companion. He shared everything. His toys. His affection. His mind! He would tell you alllll about it with his hoots and howls, whimpers and growly roars. I always looked forward to our 'talks.'

He continued to teach Phrancis the ropes and had no compunction whatsoever about putting her back in her place if she got out of hand or played too aggressive.

Phrancis settled in nicely and became a constant companion for me and Phil. She continued to give Trudy a wide berth whilst walking by, especially if there was a nugget of food on the rug. She became very protective of me and it didn't take long for me to gain her trust. She loved all the affection and attention she got, as would any dog I know.

Phil and Phrancis continued to get into trouble together. Have adventures together. And grow together.

When you looked into his eyes
you could see straight through
to his soul.

CPSIA information can be obtained
at www.ICGtesting.com
Printed in the USA
LVHW071118180222
711474LV00013B/122/J

9 780578 944777